America's PAUL REVERE

written by ESTHER FORBES *pictures by* LYND WARD
HOUGHTON MIFFLIN COMPANY · BOSTON

Printed in the United States of America

RNF ISBN 0-395-24535-4
PAP ISBN 0-395-24907-4

WOZ 10 9 8

ALL DAY Mr. Revere worked in his silver shop at the head of Clark's Wharf, Boston. He made many beautiful things — tankards and silver cups, sauce boats, buckles for gentlemen's shoes, rings for ladies' hands. And all day Mrs. Revere took care of her little house and the children. She went to market and cooked the food and washed the clothes and made new clothes and swept and scrubbed the house. The family was not rich, but they had enough. Then, when the day's work was over — and people worked from sunrise to sunset every day but Sunday — the Reveres had a little time to themselves.

So Mr. Revere would tell the children stories of his own boyhood. He had been born in a beautiful part of France called the Midi, a sunny land of vineyards. His was an ancient and respected Huguenot family who had lived in stone houses on land that they owned themselves. But the King at the time did not like the Huguenots, and if they would not change their religion to suit him, they had to leave France. Thousands left for the Dutch Lowlands, for England, and for America. Mr. Revere's parents could not leave, but they did not want their son to grow up in such a troubled country. So, when he was thirteen, and big enough to look out for himself, they sent him away, knowing they would never see him again.

Mr. Revere told his children many times how he went first to an uncle in Guernsey and then, by himself, he took a ship to America.

As they sat about the fireplace winter evenings, eating apples and cracking nuts, Mr. Revere told his children many times how he went first to an uncle living on the English island of Guernsey. But across the ocean to the west was a great continent called 'America.' Along the eastern seaboard were thirteen busy English colonies. It was a new uncrowded country and a clever boy who learned a good trade and was ready to work hard might prosper. The uncle found a ship which was going to America — so faraway, so strange a land. He paid the boy's passage and he gave the captain enough money to pay a silversmith for taking the boy into his own home and teaching him his trade. So he had come to Boston, and he had never seen his parents again. He had been homesick and frightened and lonely, and at first some of the Boston boys had laughed at his French accent. But he had learned quickly how to speak English, and he had learned the silversmith's trade. Baptized Apollos Rivoire, he changed this to Paul Revere because he found the Yankees could say it more easily. And he had given this name to his oldest son, a squarely built boy, dark-eyed and ruddy. 'Now we call the name Revere.' The father would look at his young son and smile. 'But once it was Rivoire, and in French, "rivoire" means oak.' The boy would smile back at his father. He knew his father meant, 'Take the oak as your pattern of life, for it is a strong and useful tree. There are many trees more showy than the oak, but none is so staunch, so honorable, and so good.'

Mrs. Revere, too, would tell her stories, for as they did not have any picture books, stories took their place in the Revere children's lives. Her family, the Hitchbornes, had been living about Boston almost ever since the town was a wilderness. One ancestor had been killed by the Indians and another one was a famous captain of a ship and fought the pirates.

And there were other stories, too. The children would hear of witches and demons, of Dick Whittington and his cat, of merry Robin Hood, and stories from the Bible. But by then, the little children would have been put to bed. Now all must go and be ready for work as soon as the sun rose next morning. Mrs. Revere would cover the hearth-fire with ashes. If her fire went out in the night, she would have to send Paul to a neighbor's to borrow a live coal. Mr. Revere would lock his shop and the doors of the house and perhaps let the dog in for the night and put the cat out. The father and mother slept in a big bed, a couple of small children with them. Paul and his two younger brothers had a bed in the attic, and across the hall was a bed full of sisters. The last candle was blown out, and so they slept. Then a mouse or two might peep out of their holes, timidly at first, more boldly when sure at last the cat was not at home. Soon they would scamper about looking for crumbs of corn meal the careless children had dropped at supper.

Outside, the town watch kept guard in the crowded, crooked little streets of Boston, and down the length of Clark's Wharf, just behind the Reveres' house, were ship-watchers, guarding the ships. If Paul woke in the night, he could hear the watch thumping their staves on the cobblestones, the bells of the ships telling the hour, the sea slapping idly among the piers of the wharf, or his parents snoring in the big bed. And he might hear 'squeak squeak' and a tiny rustle of little feet. Tomorrow night the cat had better sleep at home, whether she had a mind to or not.

2

When Paul was thirteen, he became an apprentice to his father, and worked all day learning to be a silversmith, even as before him his father at the same age had learned from an older smith. The apprentices worked without pay — except for food, lodging, and clothes — for seven years. Then they became master-workmen and could have shops and apprentices of their own. This was the only way skilled trades were taught.

3

For Paul, as for most boys in 1748, schooling was over by the time they were thirteen. First, Paul had gone to a dame-school where he was taught his A B C, a little reading, but not much writing. The children recited the alphabet together with 'quirks and quavers,' and were taught to bow or curtsey when spoken to and say, 'yes, ma'am,' and 'no, ma'am.' Children who did well were given cakes, but stupid children were made to stand in corners with duncecaps on their heads. Mischievous children were slapped and shaken until their teeth rattled. But such a school only cost their parents about two cents a week. When Paul was about eight, he had gone to a writing school and sat all day with the other boys on hard wooden benches. Besides writing and reading, he was taught to add and figure. Then his schooling was over. Anything more he wished to learn, he would have to teach himself, but Paul Revere went on learning all his life.

Although there were no summer vacations nor many holidays, the boys did find time to play. They had marbles and played ball games on the streets and went to the hilltops to fly their kites. Windy Beacon Hill was the best place for this. And in winter the boys coasted on the slopes of the Common, or skated on the Frog Pond. Here were — and still are — acres of land held for the use and enjoyment of the citizens. Children might play here, and here cows were pastured. On those days the militia trained on the Common, all the small boys of Boston gathered to watch. Next day they would pretend they were soldiers off to fight the Indians. The waterfront, with its ships and docks, was another favorite playground, and from the wharves in summer the boys dove and swam. But at thirteen, it was time for Paul to learn how to support himself.

Busy as he was, there were many things to do when he wasn't working.

4

When he was fifteen, Paul and six of his friends formed a 'society' to ring the bells in Christ Church. There were many fine bells in the spires of Boston churches, but none were so famous nor so fine as the eight great bells in Christ's lofty spire. Bell ringing is a skillful art, and the boys agreed to practice once a week with the trained bell-ringer and then to ring the bells whenever the wardens of the church should wish. The seven boys stood together on the second landing of the belfry. Each boy had his own great hemp rope to pull at exactly the right second. At the first peal, frightened pigeons flew in all directions from the great spire. And then the music clamored and sang until the tower itself seemed to tremble. To the farthest ends of Boston, over the water to Charlestown or Cambridge, and to the ships at sea, came the golden ringing of the bells.

Soon, in Boston, everyone who was interested in such things knew that Mr. Revere's son, Paul, although only in his teens, was such an extremely good silversmith he would in time make a really great artisan. Probably he would be more famous than his own father who had taught him. When he was eighteen, his father died, and he, as oldest son, became head of the house. It was his responsibility to see that the rent for their house and shop was paid, sometimes in money, sometimes in things he had made. After the other children had gone to bed, he and his mother would sit up to figure how best they could get along. His younger brother Thomas was also to be a silversmith and Paul would teach him. But John wanted to be a tailor. Somehow money must be saved from the shop and household to pay a master-tailor for teaching John. And the girls needed new dresses. Sometimes it was hard to see just how they could work things out. Paul loved his mother deeply, and he lived with her, or she with him, all her life.

5

Boston was a bustling, crowded, flourishing town. A great port, its wealth was in its ships. From the West Indies, the ships brought molasses and sugar, raisins, limes, and oranges. From England, they brought paper and glass, thread, fish-hooks, metal tools, and tea, coffee, silk, and spice that English ships had brought to London from the Far East. Along the wharves and in the warehouses, Paul could see these things.

6

Some of the seamen brought parrots and monkeys home with them, and all
had tales of adventure. By the time he was eighteen, there were two things
Paul could think of as he watched the ships. First, that the livelihood of
every man, woman, and child in Boston depended on the success of the ships
— and, second, that England had tax laws which, if ever enforced, would stop
much of this rich trade.

In the spring of 1756, when Paul Revere was twenty one, Massachusetts was at war and calling for volunteers. The French with their Indian allies had come down from Canada, burning farmhouses, killing men as they plowed their lonely fields, and killing or carrying away women and children. There seemed no way for the English colonies to stop this destruction except to defeat the French once and for all. France owned Canada, as England owned the colonies on the Atlantic coast. When England and France were at war in Europe, they were also fighting in the New World. The hatred between the Canadians and the New Englanders was so great that they sometimes went on fighting the French and Indian Wars, as they were called, when the mother countries were at peace in Europe. The wars were terrible and bloody, and almost every young man in Boston fought in them sooner or later.

It would be hard for Mrs. Revere, a widow with so many small children, to get along without her eldest son, who was such a clever artisan, for in the army men were paid badly or not at all. But Paul volunteered and was commissioned as a second lieutenant of artillery. He marched with the Massachusetts men to Albany, where they met troops from the other colonies who had agreed to fight the French that summer. The long trains of scarlet-and-blue-uniformed men, the creaking wagons of food, gunpowder, the slow oxen hauling guns, all turned north toward Lake George. Here at Lake George both the Americans and the French had forts. It was a wild country of forests and rushing mountain streams and great lonely swamps. For the first time, Paul heard the howling of wolves and the terrifying war-whoops of the painted savages, for the Indians usually sided with the French in these wars. They were hard to catch. Almost every day they would surprise and kill small parties of Americans.

He was a city boy, used to the smell of the sea, of the charcoal of his own shop, of the tar and spice of the waterfront. He was used to the smell of industry — the dyeing of wool, the making of leather, the brewing of ale. This far-western rim of the world, as it was then, seemed very strange to him. Yet he was able to adapt himself to whatever happened, for, from the beginning to the end of his life, he was accustomed to going ahead and doing what had to be done. He made a good soldier, for he was tireless, brave, and resourceful. Because he was generous and kind, the men who served under him liked him.

Paul spent a summer and fall fighting at Lake George. Many more men on both sides had died of sickness than of bullets, and as neither side could claim any important victory, they would continue to fight on. The Massachusetts soldiers were ordered back to Boston to be disbanded, for armies did not fight in the winter. It was a long, cold march from Lake George back to Albany and from Albany to Boston. They had only summer uniforms and the snow was already heavy. They had sick and wounded men among them, and many comrades had been left behind in shallow graves. Although not defeated, they had not been victorious.

Once more, Paul Revere went to work in his shop with his younger brother, Thomas, to help him. He was twenty-two when he came back from the wars, and he soon married Sarah Orne. But they went on living in his father's old house, with his mother and five brothers and sisters.

The French and Indian Wars went on for several more years before England sent over two of her best generals and some British troops to help the American colonies. The French were defeated, and Canada became part of the British Empire.

When the English colonies no longer feared attack from the north, people dared settle farther inland, even places as far away and as wild as Kentucky were being settled. For some years, the British had been buying supplies in Boston for their soldiers and sailors in America. Farming and shipping and manufacturing had all grown, to meet the demands of war. Although many families were sorrowing for men who had been killed, people on the whole were prosperous and could afford to buy fine silver. Paul Revere continued to live in his little house at the head of Clark's Wharf and to make his famous silver.

But suddenly this prosperity was over, and there was a bad depression. England, who had the largest empire the world had ever seen, was also feeling very poor, and she had no idea how to govern her vast possessions. The colonies had always agreed that England had the right to control their shipping and to collect money from them, but she had been too busy fighting to bother. Now, at peace, England decided to enforce old laws, pass new ones, and to collect the customs. Boston had been sending her ships where she pleased. She was angry that England now intended to make her obey the laws — laws made in London. No American had had a chance to vote on these laws.

Both England and the American colonies thought there should be a British army of ten thousand regulars kept in America as protection against the Indians. But who was to pay for them? England insisted that the colonies pay, and because the customs officials could not get enough money for the army by taxing shipping, she decided to tax something else. So the English Parliament passed a 'Stamp Act.' This meant that all papers, such as marriage certificates, mortgages, or bills of sale, had to have a stamp on them before they were legal. Even newspapers could not be sold without a stamp. This was the first direct tax upon the people, and all up and down the eastern seaboard, men sprang to their feet and cried that the colonies must never agree to any tax unless they could select the men for Parliament who voted these taxes. 'Taxation without representation is tyranny.' There were no colonists in the British Parliament when the stamp tax was passed.

The night it was known that ships carrying the stamps would arrive, the colonists were ready for them. In Boston, hundreds of men and boys had been told to stand ready to protest and by their determination and numbers to frighten the officials. Paul Revere, one of the leaders knew what was going to be done that night. A great stuffed dummy, or effigy, of the Boston official whose business it was to distribute the stamps was to be hung on a tree. There was also an effigy for Lord Bute, the Englishman who had proposed the tax in Parliament. He was represented by a gigantic boot with a devil peeking out of it. All the next day the effigies hung, and at night the colonists made a bonfire of them. From that day on, the great elm from which the effigies were hung was called 'The Tree of Liberty,' and the men who organized this protest were called 'Sons of Liberty.'

10

Up and down the coast, hundreds of towns selected some stately tree and called it their 'Liberty Tree.' People gathered to meet under them and to swear, 'taxation without representation is tyranny.' The last thing they wanted was to fight their mother country, for most of the people were English and proud of it. But unless England stopped taxing the colonies without giving them a place in Parliament, they would fight.

Still, times were bad and money scarce. Paul Revere had been married now for nine years and had five children. The oldest, Debby, was eight. Then came Paul, Jr., Sara, Mary, and Fanny, the baby. As his mother lived with him, he had eight people to feed and clothe. Everyone in Boston was hard up — from the great merchants down to the poorest porters. As silver was an expensive luxury, Paul had to find something else to sell, something everyone could afford, so he decided to take up another trade. Although it was difficult, Revere was such a skilled craftsman that he taught himself to engrave copper plates. From these plates, he printed pictures on pieces of paper, and they were sold on the street for only a few pennies each. Many of them were hand-colored. Sometimes he made plates to illustrate books and, later, for magazines. There were other engravers in Boston who were more skillful than he, but none whose work reflected so clearly what people were thinking. He made many political cartoons, among them a picture of the effigies hanging from the Liberty Tree. When England failed in her efforts to collect money from the American colonies, Revere's quick eye always noticed. He made cartoons of England's attempts to enforce taxes, and then even those who could not read could understand the situation.

He also learned dentistry. Nobody knew then how to fill teeth. If a tooth ached, it was pulled out — and often instruments, as well as jaws, were broken in the process. Nearly everyone over twenty had already lost one or more teeth. How to make false ones and fasten them in was a secret few people knew, but Revere learned from an Englishman who happened to be in Boston how to carve teeth from ivory or to use an animal's tooth. Usually a sheep's tooth was selected as not being of 'too peculiar form.' These were fastened in the mouth with silver wires.

12

Here is one of Paul Revere's advertisements: *Whereas many Persons are so unfortunate as to lose their Fore-teeth by Accident, and otherways, to their great Detriment not only in Looks but speaking both in Public and Private: — This is to inform all such that they may have them replaced with artificial ones, that looks as well as Natural, & answeres the End of Speaking to all intents, by PAUL REVERE, Goldsmith, near the Head of Dr. Clark's Wharf, Boston.*

A few years later, after he learned more, Revere advertised that he fixed teeth 'in such a Manner that they were not only an Ornament, but of real use in Speaking and Eating.' He practiced dentistry for only a few years, nor did he make copper plates very long, for in neither of these trades did he excel, nor did they seem to interest him.

As artisans worked from sunup to sundown, Revere was very busy, for, besides his trade, he belonged to a number of political clubs. Boston was dividing into two groups, the Tories and the Whigs. The Tories believed England had every right to tax them, and that the colonies would be better off to be always a part of the powerful British Empire. Paul Revere and the men who thought as he did were called Whigs or Patriots. They thought the American colonies were now strong enough to get along without the protection of the British fleet and the British army, and that England should not meddle with their laws. The colonies had more democratic forms of government than England, and did not want the mother country upsetting their new system. Above all, they did not want to be taxed. Sam Adams and James Otis were leaders of the Whigs in Boston, and John Adams, John Hancock, and Josiah Quincy all were important Patriots. These men were Paul Revere's friends, and he often met secretly with them in garrets and back rooms of taverns, planning the future of the country.

Not all Paul Revere's friends were Whigs. One of them, John Singleton Copley, was a Tory and a Boston artist who painted the best portraits in America. He often went to Revere's shop, as Revere made the delicate gold frames for the tiny miniatures he painted on ivory. One day, when Copley was in the shop, Revere went through his ledgers to count up how much was owed for his gold frames. It was quite a sum — just about the amount Copley charged for his oil portraits. So it was decided that he would paint Revere's portrait in payment for his bill.

Usually, the men and women who posed for Copley wore their best clothes. They were people of fashion and importance, and dressed in judges' gowns or black clericals, in magnificent satins, or velvet laces, the ladies decked out with ribbons and feathers. He painted many famous lawyers, merchants, doctors, or political leaders like Sam Adams, but very few artisans.

Paul Revere was proud to be a silversmith, so he did not go home to powder his hair, as was the fashion then, and put on his best clothes. He did not even put on his coat. Copley set up his easel and began to mix his paint, while Paul went on working at the teapot he happened to be making. Copley studied his friend's face, noticed the generous width between the eyes, the bold turn of the mouth, the quizzical lift of the eyebrow. He noticed how delicate his fingers were, and how thick and strong his wrists. Although he might not approve of his friend's politics, he approved of the man.

14

So he painted Paul Revere just as he appeared at his workbench in his work clothes with the tools of his trade about him — 'Bold Revere,' as his friends called him, cool in thought, ardent in action.' All this shows in the face Copley painted, as well as his generosity and courage. Copley painted not only what Revere looked like, but his character and the principles he stood for.

Because the British customs officials were not allowed by the Sons of Liberty to collect tax money, they begged England to send them soldiers to enforce the law. So two regiments of regulars arrived in Boston. They must have been unusually bad-tempered fellows, as they were always having quarrels and fist-fights with the citizens, who hated them and amused themselves by tripping them and calling them, because of their scarlet uniforms, 'lobsters,' or 'bloody-backs,' and worse names. Small boys followed them on the street, yelling, 'lobsters for sale.'

As Paul Revere watched this continual scuffling between the inhabitants and the regulars, he knew, as did the other leaders in Boston, that sometime something worse than scuffles was bound to happen. Sometime, the soldiers would be so hard-pressed or so angry they would fire upon the people. Sometime people were going to be killed. It was a year and a half after the troops arrived that this happened.

Snow fell that day — March 5, 1770. 'Ah,' thought Revere, looking out of his shop window. 'The weather is bad enough to keep both soldiers and townsfolk indoors today. People don't riot in snowstorms.'

At noon, the snow stopped. By evening, the soldiers, more evil-tempered than ever and the townspeople more insulting than usual, were crowding each other on the street, calling names, making threats. Excitement grew all over Boston, for everybody knew that there had been some ugly street-fights lately. It was like sitting on gunpowder.

Paul Revere probably did what most of the wiser citizens of Boston did that night. He stayed off the streets, and was already in bed when he first heard the whistling and yelling and the cry, 'Town-born turn out! Town-born turn out!'

Church bells began clanging furiously, from one end of town to the other.

'What's up?' He already had his head out the window.

'The British regulars are massacring the inhabitants. Slashing and killing every way,' a voice cried.

'They are cutting down our Liberty Tree.'

'No . . . it's only a fire. Grab your fire bucket and come, Revere.'

It was true the bells were ringing exactly as they would for a fire. Revere dressed and joined the people, some carrying firebuckets and others swords and pistols, running toward Kings Street. And there, in the moonlight, he saw what had happened.

A barber's boy had insulted a British officer in front of the State House. The solitary sentry had knocked the child down. People had been throwing chunks of ice and insults at this sentry for some time, and he was in bad temper.

The boy was not hurt, but the cry went up that the bloody butcher had killed him, and the people close to the sentry yelled, 'Kill him! Kill him!' More and more people had come running to see what had happened. Fire bells had begun to ring.

16

The sentry called for help. Captain Preston and seven privates had come to his rescue, but the people were not afraid of nine British soldiers. They pushed against them, knocked down one soldier, hit Captain Preston with a cudgel. When the soldiers threatened to fire, they told them to go ahead, until at last they had fired. There on the trampled snow lay four men dead. The eight wounded were still struggling and crying out.

17

It was Crispus Attucks, an enormous man, part Negro, part Indian, and part white, who had struck Captain Preston and knocked down the British soldier, Montgomery. He was shot. Sam Gray had had a fight with another of the soldiers, Kilroy, a few days before. Each was determined to kill the other one when he could. Now Kilroy saw his chance and Gray died at the soldier's feet. But neither James Caldwell nor the boy, Sam Maverick, seem to have been in the actual attack. They were killed by stray bullets.

The soldiers stood huddled together, their smoking muskets still in their hands. Now through the hubbub of bells and shouting came the roll of British drums. Both regiments were being called out to keep what order they might for the rest of the night.

Before morning, Captain Preston and his eight men were in jail, charged with murder. And in a few days they were the only soldiers left in Boston. The town insisted the others be sent away, and they were.

Then Paul Revere was asked to draw a diagram of exactly what he had seen that night. It was to be used in the trial of the soldiers and would show where they stood and where the people they had killed fell. But he, like most of Boston, was very angry to think the soldiers had fired on the citizens. He was angry that soldiers had even been sent there in the first place. After he had finished his accurate diagram, he decided to do a print which would make other people as angry as he was. This is the most famous of all American prints, but it did, as was later said at the trial, 'add wings to fancy.' It was not supposed to show what really happened, as his diagram did, but to infuriate his fellow citizens. In the print, the inhabitants are not knocking down soldiers, but standing about very innocently, merely serving as targets. And Captain Preston is not risking his life to prevent his men from firing a second time, but urging them on with his sword.

Besides the three men and one boy who were killed instantly, one of the wounded died four days later. This was a young Irish leather-breeches-maker, Patrick Carr. To the end, he protested that the soldiers fired in self-defense. If they had not, they would have been killed. He did not blame them for his agonizing death. This dying statement of Patrick Carr made the angry people stop and think. Were the soldiers really guilty of murder? Or did they fire in self-defense?

At first no lawyer could be found who dared defend them. They were afraid they would be mobbed or killed. But two of the Patriots finally agreed to do so. John Adams, later the second President of the United States, and Josiah Quincy felt it would be a disgrace forever if men accused of murder could not get a fair trial in the courts. Three people, therefore, came through the Boston Massacre with great honor. The poor unknown Irish man who insisted upon telling the truth, and the two famous lawyers who risked their reputations and popularity to defend the hated British soldiers. Montgomery and Kilroy were found guilty of manslaughter. The others were innocent. With no regulars left on the streets of Boston, life seemed quite normal again.

18

And in London on the very day of the Massacre, Parliament voted not to make the American colonists pay any duties on anything except one small thing. There still was a little tax on tea. This was hardly more than a symbol that Parliament had not given up her claim to tax the colonies as she chose, for that was her business. The colonists still insisted that it was their business.

Paul Revere's life went quietly for three years. True, there was that tax on tea, and most patriotic people refused to buy it from England. They drank tea smuggled from Holland or went without. In London, the great East India Company was almost in bankruptcy, although her warehouses were full of tea, and it was decided this tea must be sold in America to save the company. The tax to the Government would be paid in England, and the tea would be sold in America very cheaply. Thus, the British Government hoped to make the Americans forget they were being taxed — and without representation. Yet, if the colonists bought the tea, it would be an admission that England had the right to tax them. It might begin with only this tiny tax, but it could end anywhere — taxes on houses and farms, ships and shops. It was not for the sake of their pocketbooks the colonists decided to resist the tax, but for the principle involved.

Late in 1773, word came that three ships full of tea had left London and were heading for Boston. One of them, the *Dartmouth*, arrived at Griffin Wharf on the twenty-ninth of November. A great mass meeting of all citizens was called. It was decided the tea must never be unloaded, and a guard was stationed at Griffin Wharf to see that none of it was taken ashore. That night, Paul Revere was one of the men who guarded the *Dartmouth*. If the other two ships, the *Eleanor* and the *Beaver*, heard of the cold welcome awaiting them in Boston they might put in at one of the smaller Massachusetts ports, Salem or Gloucester or Plymouth, so riders were sent out the next night to warn the other towns. Paul Revere had been up all one night guarding the *Dartmouth* — the next night he was flying over frozen roads and through darkness, with the warning.

'You've heard the news? The *Dartmouth's* in Boston. We've sworn she'll never unload her tea on *us*. You feel the same way, sir? Watch out then for the *Eleanor* and the *Beaver*. We've got to stand together in this.'

Soon these two ships joined the *Dartmouth* at Griffin Wharf. They had on board 342 great chests of tea. All day and night a guard of citizens stood watch, allowing them to unload everything except the hated tea. Almost every day, there were mass meetings at Old South Church. The law said that if a ship did not unload within twenty days, its cargo would be seized and sold at auction. This, the people of Boston were determined, never should happen. They demanded that the ships be sent back to England. But legally no ship could leave a port unless it had unloaded, and the only person who could give it permission to do so was Governor Hutchinson, who stayed out in the country, well away from the rising passions of Boston. The mass meetings sent request after request to him to permit the ships to sail. He refused.

On the sixteenth of December, the *Dartmouth* had been in for nineteen days. On the next day her cargo would be unloaded and sold. The leaders, Sam Adams, John Hancock, Joseph Warren, and Paul Revere, knew what would happen if the Governor still refused, so secretly, they told perhaps a hundred and fifty boys and young men to be all ready with disguises and axes.

20

That evening, in kitchens and shops and back rooms of taverns, men and boys were dressing in blankets and work-smocks, in old dresses of their mothers, smudging their faces with black soot or red paint, waiting for the signal. Some stuck feathers in their caps and called themselves 'Mohawks.' They agreed to talk only in Indian grunts, for it must never be known who they were. With the group at the Green Dragon was Paul Revere.

While the masqueraders dressed, a mass meeting was still going on in Old South Church. Thousands stood outside in the street, waiting for Mr. Rotch, the owner of the ships, to come back for the last time from begging the Governor to let them return to England. Mr. Rotch came back defeated, and Sam Adams dismissed the meeting with the quiet words, 'This meeting can do nothing more to save the country.'

These words were the signal. Indian whoops and hoops, yells of 'Boston Harbor, a teapot tonight!' 'To Griffin Wharf!' 'To Griffin Wharf!' 'Salt water tea!' But if one ounce of tea was stolen, the 'tea party' would be a robbery and not a protest.

Three parties of 'Indians,' one of them under the command of Paul Revere, silently boarded the three tea ships.

All Boston moved down onto Griffin Wharf, and in bright moonlight watched the men hoist the heavy chests up on deck and with their axes break each one open and dump the tea in Boston Harbor. Hardly a word was said. It took hours to do this work. Not one thing except the tea was injured. They were so careful that a padlock one of the boys broke by mistake was replaced, and when they had finished dumping the tea, they borrowed brooms and swept the decks. Nobody would ever be able to say the Boston Tea Party was the work of a crazy mob. Not a leaf of tea was stolen.

It was long after midnight when Paul Revere got home to his little house in North Square that night. He, like the other Indians, was tired, for the work had been hard. It was easier to put paint and soot on his face than to take it off. Yet hardly had he cleaned off his disguise than he was asked to saddle and ride instantly. Both New York and Philadelphia were expecting tea ships, and so also was Charleston in South Carolina. Revere was asked to ride as fast as he could to New York and Philadelphia, and tell them what Boston had done.

While he was away, there appeared among the shops and taverns and wharves a song honoring him and Joseph Warren and the part they and the old Green Dragon Tavern had played in the tea party. Bohea was one of the best grades of tea.

'Rally, Mohawks! Bring out your axes
And tell King George we'll pay no taxes
    On his foreign tea;
His threats are vain, and vain to think
To force our girls and wives to drink
    His vile Bohea!
Then rally, boys, and hasten on
To meet our chiefs at the Green Dragon.

'Our Warren's there, and bold Revere
With hands to do, and words to cheer
    For Liberty and laws:
Our Country's 'braves' and true defenders
Shall ne'er be left by true North-enders
    Fighting Freedom's call.
Then rally, boys, and hasten on
To meet our chiefs at the Green Dragon '

Other men might stay home and sing songs and rest up from the night's hard work, but for Paul Revere there was no rest. In those days of winding roads it was seven hundred miles from Boston to Philadelphia and back, a long and lonely ride to take in wintertime. Revere changed horses often and rode hard, for he was back again in Boston in eleven days, much more quickly than anyone thought possible.

25

The news which Revere brought back from Philadelphia was good. Both in New York and Philadelphia, people thought Boston had been right to destroy the tea. They would see to it none was landed down upon them. And if England punished Boston for her Tea Party, they promised to stand by her, for everyone knew that some way, somehow, England would try to make Boston pay for the tea. Because of the disguise the Tea Party Mohawks had worn, it would never be known who the men and boys were. It was useless trying to find out and bring them to trial. No one would ever tell.

A ship, carrying the news to London about the tea party, took a month to make the voyage. And Parliament took about a month to argue and make up its mind. Then, a month for another ship to get back to Boston. It was not until May that His Majesty's ship, *The Lively*, dropped anchor in Boston Harbor with orders for the town's punishment. Until the tea was paid for, no ship, nor boat — not even a scow carrying in firewood, or a ferry crossing to Charlestown — could leave or enter Boston.

This punishment was greater than anyone had imagined possible. Boston's entire livelihood depended upon her ships. Rich merchants, owners of great wharves, and sea captains would be ruined first, but so would the sailors who manned the ships, the porters who loaded them, the draymen who carted away the cargoes. No one would be able to afford a new suit, and the tailors would shut up shop. The tailors would not buy cloth, and the clothiers would be ruined. Paul Revere would have fewer orders for silver. People might not be able even to get food or fuel, for such things had in the past usually come to Boston by water. The town was almost an island, as only one little bad road connected it with the mainland. Hundreds of frightened people left Boston for the country. They were afraid of starvation and riots. Some of the leaders of the Tea Party Indians decided it was not safe for them, but Paul Revere was not afraid. He stayed.

Parliament had decided that from now on, until Boston paid for the tea, Salem was to be the capital of the colony. Governor Hutchinson was to go back to England to report, and his place would be taken by General Gage. He was an English army man, and it was thought he would be stricter than the Boston-born Hutchinson.

Hardly had this news come than Revere was again in the saddle, to take once more the long ride to New York and Philadelphia with the story of Boston's plight. But it was May now, not bleak December. The apple trees were in blossom and the birds singing. Everywhere he went, he found the Patriots united as never before. For if Boston was to be starved into submission, why not Charleston next, or Philadelphia, New York, or Baltimore? By the time he was back once more, he found that the British fleet and transports carrying hundreds of regulars were already arriving. It was their business to see that Parliament's orders were carried out, to close the port of Boston until the town voted to pay for the tea. The Boston Port Bill was to be strictly enforced.

Paul Revere saw men and women, boys and girls, angrily watching transports unloading British troops. At the time of the Boston Massacre, there were only two regiments, not enough to keep the King's peace. Parliament would not make that mistake again. Before summer was over, when Paul Revere walked down the streets of his town, he noticed every third person he met was a British regular. Boston was flooded with scarlet uniforms.

Until now the thirteen colonies along the Atlantic coast had not done much about sticking together. Each colony had thought first of its own welfare, before considering that of the twelve other colonies. England knew this when passing the Boston Port Bill, she had counted on their inability to unite. Now they were united as never before. The citizens did not plague the regulars this time, for there were too many of them. The town was quite orderly.

Boston did not starve. Towns all through New England sent her food — codfish and corn and livestock and rye, and even sheep from Connecticut. Charleston sent loads of rice and Baltimore quantities of bread. All these things had to come into the town, in great drays and wagons, over the one road which connected Boston with the mainland, for nothing could come by ship.

Some towns sent money. Far off in London, money was raised for the people of Boston, for there were many in England who sympathized with America, and were against King George III, his cabinet, and the majority party in Parliament. They felt that the Whigs in America were struggling to preserve English liberties. The struggle between England and the colonies was never neatly divided, with all the English on one side and all the Americans on the other.

Many Americans who were Tories thought England was right. Many Englishmen believed in the colonies' cause. Families were divided: one brother on one side; another on the other. Sometimes a wife was a Tory and her husband a Whig. Many people did not know which side they were on. Paul Revere always knew. But even though he was a Whig, many of his friends were Tories. He was a friendly man and it probably bothered him that now when he went to walk on the Common with his children, some old friends did not speak to him. And some said ugly things.

'Hm . . . Mr. Revere. You Son of Liberty — Son of Perdition. I'll live to see you hang, sir. Hang for treason.'

And off this old 'friend' would stalk with his nose in the air.

Revere would try to explain to his children, as best he could, the great principles of freedom and democracy for which he stood.

'Papa, why is Mr. Joy so mad?'

'He's a Tory, son, and I'm a Whig.'

'He used to be our friend.'

'Not now. Not any more.'

Then a file of scarlet British drummers would come prancing over the Common rolling their drums, their drumsticks falling in perfect time. The children would skip for joy in time to the music. But Revere would turn away his eyes.

'Papa, don't you like to hear the British drummers?'

'I hate the sound. It means there will be war. Every decent man hates war. But sometimes it can't be helped!'

28

Very big, very red, very burly, these soldiers looked to the small children of Boston. And now there were so many of them! You could hardly turn around without bumping into a soldier. General Gage moved eleven regiments with all their equipment into Boston that summer. The first thing you heard in the morning was the rattle of their drums. The last thing at night was the clumping of their heavy army boots.

Now, when Paul Revere and his children finished their walk, they did not go home to Clark's Wharf, but to their new home in North Square. About the time of the Boston Massacre, Revere had bought a tiny brown house already about a hundred years old, very solidly built, flush on the street. It still stands in Boston as a memorial to him. In the huge back yard was a stable where the horse was kept. There was room for the children to play and for cats and dogs and pigs, and room, too, for the new Mrs. Revere's clothesline, for the children's mother had died and their father had married again. They loved their stepmother very much. Their grandmother also lived with them. It was a crowded, happy little house. In one way they were lucky to be so crowded. They had no spare bed. For wherever there was a spare bed in Boston, the British officers were apt to tuck in a few soldiers. Other families around North Square, who had bigger houses than the Reveres, or a smaller number of children, had soldiers living with them.

Paul Revere's workshop was still down at Clark's Wharf. His oldest boy, Paul, had always wanted to be a silversmith, like his father and grandfather before him. Soon he would be through his schooling and be in the shop all day, learning the family trade.

Before so many British regulars arrived, Paul Revere had often stuck a cockade in his hat, and hung a medal around his neck. On one side of the medal was engraved a tree of liberty, and on the other side a liberty cap. Then he would be off marching, with thousands of other Sons of Liberty. Now they could have no more of these marches and great feasts, or demonstrations like hanging effigies on the Liberty Tree. General Gage and his redcoats were in Boston to stop them. So the Sons of Liberty had to form more and more secret little clubs. Such clubs kept few records of what they said or did, or even of their membership. They were too close to treason, for which the members could be sent to London to be hanged. But General Gage believed that as time went on, the spirit of rebellion would die down. He did not want to hang men, such as Sam Adams or Joseph Warren or John Hancock or James Otis, to make the people more angry than they were. The thirteen colonies had always quarreled among themselves. He'd wait until they started in again.

Although the Whigs still protested in public and in newspapers, they met secretly in small groups, trying to figure out what they could do to make

Parliament recall the British troops, let their ships sail once more, and take the tax off tea. They realized it was important to keep in touch with the Whig leaders in the other colonies, to be really united. So they formed Committees of Correspondence in all the colonies to send letters back and forth. It was not safe to trust these letters to the ordinary mail, and Paul Revere was often asked to carry them.

Although some of the Whigs left Boston because they were afraid of the British soldiers, many Tories from other towns came to live in Boston because they were afraid of the Whigs. In those other towns, where there were no troops to protect them, they were often insulted and attacked by angry groups who even threatened to kill them. Many refugees who ran to General Gage for protection were rich and prominent. Others were poor. All of them were sure that the British army would march out of Boston soon, put down the rebellion, and then they could go home again.

General Gage found himself in a strange position in Boston. He had a good little army. All day his soldiers drilled and drilled. Here he was cock o' the walk. The King told him to go ahead and arrest the rebellious leaders, but if he did, 'the country would rush in' and kill all his soldiers. At that time, anyone, with a musket good enough to shoot ducks and a knife sharp enough to cut up leather for shoes, was about as well-armed as any soldier. General Gage knew that in the country thousands of men were drilling. They were collecting ammunition, muskets, and cannon, selecting officers. These armed farmers promised each other that if they ever were needed to fight the regulars, they would answer the alarm in a minute. Therefore, they were called Minute Men.

So, while Gage was drilling his fine white-and-scarlet regulars in Boston, these very irregular farmers were drilling without uniforms or military smartness in all the country towns. Gage would never dare just march out of Boston with flags flying and drums rolling and seize the colonists' military supplies now. He would have to be quick and sly about it — strike before the Minute Men had time to gather. He knew the Americans were good soldiers even if they did not have handsome uniforms.

In 1774, the First Continental Congress was held in Philadelphia. All the Revere family gathered with the rest of the townspeople to watch the Massachusetts delegates, among whom were Sam Adams and John Adams, leaving Boston. They did not go secretly, but in a coach and four which drove past the five regiments camped on Boston Common as if daring the British to arrest them. At Philadelphia, the delegates from all the colonies argued how far they should go in resisting. Not even these Whig leaders of all the colonies could agree.

Massachusetts was afraid that she might become involved in a war with the entire British Empire without the other twelve colonies doing a thing to help her. While this first Congress was sitting, Paul Revere arrived with some 'resolves' which had been drawn up in Massachusetts. If they were adopted, Massachusetts would not have to fight alone. Tired as Paul Revere was by the long hard ride from Boston to Philadelphia, he would not rest until he found out how this, our first Congress, would vote. Would they pass the Suffolk Resolves? He knew it was said in them that Massachusetts felt 'no obedience is due from this promise to England.' The Suffolk Resolves were passed. If the British soldiers in Boston did the attacking, the twelve other colonies would come to Massachusetts' help, but if Boston attacked the soldiers, they would not. Many at that Congress felt it was almost a declaration of war. And 'grave pacific old Quakers' sat in their chairs in Carpenter's Hall with tears running down their faces.

Few Americans wanted to fight with England, but they did want justice and representative government for themselves and their children. They wanted America to become a great and happy nation, and they were ready to fight that generations to come after them might be free.

33

People did not have long to wonder if Gage's little army would be content to sit in Boston doing nothing. Soon, very cautiously, Gage sent out a small party to seize military supplies at Charlestown. They got the powder and were off again before the Minute Men knew they had started. Patriots realized there had to be some system set up in Boston to find out in advance where and when the British intended to attack, to spread the alarm and call out the Minute Men.

Paul Revere wrote how that winter he 'was one of upwards of thirty, chiefly mechanics, who formed ourselves into a comittee for the purpose of watching the movements of the British soldiers and gaining every intelligence of the movement of the Tories. We held our meetings at the Green Dragon. . . . In winter toward spring we frequently took turns, two and two, to watch the soldiers, by patrolling the streets all night.' It was through this spy system that Revere received word the British planned to send reinforcements to the fort at Portsmouth, New Hampshire. Revere rode to near-by Durham and warned the Patriots. They seized a British fort and the King's gunpowder before the regulars even left Boston. That expedition was given up, and the fighting did not begin at Portsmouth.

By patrolling the streets and keeping eyes and ears open, the Patriots could tell pretty well when any redcoats were being sent out of Boston. But Gage had one regiment on Castle Island in the harbor. Paul Revere might walk the streets of town without anyone suspecting him. It was quite another thing to patrol Castle Island in a rowboat. One dark night, he and five other men were trying to do exactly this, when the British caught them. They could not explain what they were doing, rowing in the middle of the night, and were locked up on Castle Island. During the night, they could hear the regiment getting on boats. They could hear people yelling that they were going to Salem and seize the rebels' supplies there. Colonel Leslie was going with them. There was not one thing the six prisoners could do. It looked as if Colonel Leslie was going to get what he was after, and not a Minute Man would be warned in time.

So Colonel Leslie went to Salem and made his famous 'retreat.' When he got there, word had spread fast that 'the regulars are out.' The angry people and great numbers of armed farmers arrived so quickly he gave up the idea of seizing supplies and put his men back on their ships to return to Castle Island. So the fighting did not begin at Salem.

Doubtless, Paul Revere and his friends felt very discouraged that night. The spy system had not worked. As soon as the regulars were home again, Revere and his companions were allowed to get in their boat and row back to Boston. But from then on, they perfected their system. A British officer could hardly sneeze without someone reporting it to Paul Revere or Joseph Warren.

But while the Patriots were spying on the British to keep track of what they were up to, the British spied on the Yankees. General Gage sent out one or two of his soldiers dressed like Yankee farmers. They walked around through

34

the country, asking if anyone would like to hire them.   One pretended to be a gunsmith, and actually worked on guns which people said they were getting in good order so they could shoot at 'that flock of redcoats' in Boston if ever they left the safety of town.   They found out easily where the Yankees were keeping their supplies, and discovered one of the most important collections of gunpowder, muskets, and even cannon, was at Concord.

Always on March fifth, there was a big mass meeting to commemorate the Boston Massacre. It was held in Old South Church and orations were given. These were violently anti-British. It had been tyranny five years before to land two regiments down on Boston — and naturally bloodshed had been the result. Now, in 1775, there were six times as many soldiers — the tyranny six times as bad. Most people suspected that more blood soon would be shed. People were saying Gage would prohibit the meeting, but he did not. Then they said he was waiting to get all the most prominent Whigs in one building and arrest them all. They were not arrested. But some of his young officers decided to attend and interrupt the speakers and make what trouble they could. But people treated them politely, and the meeting went off without any violence. Paul Revere's close friend, Doctor Joseph Warren, was the orator that year. And Sam Adams and John Hancock both sat on the platform. It took courage for them to appear publicly and denounce British rule. This meeting should be remembered as an example of 'freedom of speech.' What was said was close to treason. Any time he wanted, Gage could arrest the leaders and send them to London. King George was angry that he did not, and there was a rhyme the British soldiers liked:

> As for their King John Hancock
> And Adams, if they're taken,
> Their heads for signs shall hang on high
> Upon that hill called "Beacon." '

Soon afterward both Adams and Hancock left Boston. Joseph Warren and Paul Revere stayed on.

36

And so it was the eighteenth of April in the year seventeen-seventy-five. People wondered if this was the day General Gage would send out his men to seize John Hancock and Sam Adams, who were at Lexington, and capture the military supplies the Patriots had hidden at Concord and other inland towns. The spy system reported that the British were preparing boats, and that six hundred of the best of the regulars were being held ready for *something*. Was it for an attack?

Paul Revere had suggested that if the regulars left by land, one lantern would be shown in the spire of Christ Church. If by sea, two. The British would try to stop all messengers from Boston who might warn the Minute Men However, two men would try to get out. One was Billy Dawes, who would leave by the town gate. The other, Paul Revere, who would, if he did not get caught, cross the Charles River to Charlestown.

That afternoon he saw that the *Somerset*, British man-o'-war, was being moved into the mouth of the Charles to stop people like himself who might want to cross the river. As soon as it was dark, from all over Boston, groups of British regulars marched stealthily toward the foot of the Common and got into boats. At ten o'clock, Joseph Warren sent word for Billy Dawes to start, and Paul Revere told Robert Newman to show two lanterns in the steeple. If neither he nor Dawes got past the British, the lanterns would at least give some warning.

When he had sent Newman off, he went home to say goodbye to his family and get his riding boots. North Square, where he lived, was already full of troops, waiting to march. He was careful that no one saw what he was doing.

Two of Revere's friends rowed him over to Charlestown.

Charlestown had seen the tiny lights in the steeple. The Patriots there were expecting Revere, and had a fast horse saddled and waiting. Revere flung himself on the horse, and so alone down the dark road and through the bright white moonlight he rode to spread the alarm. At Lexington, John Hancock and Sam Adams were staying with the Clarks. He wished to warn them they might be seized for high treason. He later said that at Medford, 'I

alarmed the Captain of the Minute Men, and after that I alarmed almost every house till I got to Lexington. Up flew windows and out popped heads. ''The regulars are out.'' ' ' ''What? How's that?'' ' ' ''The regulars are out.'' '

Bells rang and drums beat. Men mounted and galloped off to warn other towns. Minute Men jumped from their beds, grabbed muskets, and hastened to the rendezvous.

It was midnight, when Revere woke John Hancock and Sam Adams to tell them the regulars were out and they had best hide themselves. Half an hour later, Dawes arrived. The two messengers ate together, rested their horses, and decided to continue to Concord. Everyone knew Concord had a large supply of military equipment. The Sunday before, Revere had told them they had better begin hiding it, because in Boston people thought the regulars would soon try to capture the supplies. Young Doctor Prescott said he would go with them. The three left Lexington together. One would stop and knock at one door, and another at the next. By now, they knew that General Gage had sent out, very secretly the day before, a number of British officers, who, as soon as the regulars left Boston, were to hide in the bushes along the roads leading to Concord and stop all messengers. Revere had already met two of them when he left Charlestown, but his fast Yankee horse had quickly left them behind. When the three men were only halfway to Concord, they met another group of officers. Paul Revere was on the road. They jumped out of the darkness at him with drawn pistols almost before he saw them, but he had time to call a warning to Dawes and Prescott, who were knocking at farmhouse doors. An officer raced to catch them, but Dawes broke through and fell off his horse. Doctor Prescott jumped a wall and was off for Concord, leaving no danger that Concord would be surprised. The Minute Men were well aroused. It was the group of ten British officers who were in danger of being captured by the Minute Men if they did not quickly join the British troops come out from Boston.

They questioned Revere.

'How far is Cambridge? What is your name?'

'Revere.'

'What, *Paul* Revere?'

They knew they had caught Boston's most famous express rider. Soon they let the other men whom they had picked up that night go, and hurried as fast as they could for Lexington, hoping to join the troops. A sergeant led Revere's horse. An officer kept a pistol pointed at his head.

'If you attempt to run or we are insulted, we'll blow out your brains,' he said.

'You may do as you please,' Revere said. He knew his mission was accomplished.

But when the British found they had to hurry, they could not bother with a prisoner. They took Revere's horse away and let him go free. As he was already in Lexington, he decided to go to the Clarks' parsonage and see if he could help Hancock and Adams. He found they were just leaving, and went with them. Then Hancock remembered he had left a trunk full of papers, which must not fall into the hands of the British, at Buchman Tavern on Lexington Green, so Revere and Hancock's clerk went back to save them. In Lexington, there was great excitement. People said the British regulars were very close. Revere saw the thin line of Minute Men standing on the Green waiting for them. He and the clerk hurried to the tavern. As they were carrying the trunk out of the tavern door, they saw the scarlet flood of British regulars come to a halt before the handful of Minute Men. The British officers galloped ahead to order the Minute Men to disperse. Revere walked through the lines carrying his half of the dangerous trunk. He heard a shot and then a volley, cries of wounded men, and the huzzahing of the exultant troops, passing through the handful of men who thought to oppose them, as they headed now for Concord. The first shot of the American Revolution had been fired.

During the Revolution, Paul Revere was a lieutenant colonel of artillery. Most of the time, after the British were driven out of Boston, he was in command of Castle Island. As he walked about the ramparts, he must often have thought of how he and his five fellow spies had once been locked up in this same fort. After the war started, there was not much fighting around Boston. Revere did go on two expeditions to drive the British out of Newport, Rhode Island, and one to the Penobscot in Maine, but these campaigns were heartbreaking and unsuccessful.

After six and a half years of fighting, peace came at last. The colonies had won their freedom, but were very poor, and still not well united. Besides making silver after the war, Revere sold other things imported from England, at his shop, eyeglasses and wallpaper, fine sealing wax and playing cards, and better cloth than could be woven in America. People were famished for such luxuries. He also sold much hardware, and soon, instead of importing it, he began to make it himself. Boston and her wealth still depended on her great merchant ships. Now for the first time American ships were venturing far out into the Pacific — to India, China, and Java — bringing back silks, tea, coffee, and spice. These were wooden ships, but they were put together with metal. Revere usually made parts for ships, of copper. No one else in America knew how to work copper as well as he did. With no one to teach him, he experimented and found out for himself.

Young America had not a friend in the world, nor a single warship. France and the Algerian pirates both were attacking American merchantmen and England was still angry. It was decided the country had to have a navy. Revere did much work on these ships, and eventually he learned how to roll the copper into sheets to be used for sheathing their bottoms. Until he found out how to do this, all the copper sheathing came from Europe, and any war could cut off the supply. Very few people knew how to do this in Europe, and no one else over here. Perhaps the greatest service Paul Revere ever did for his country was this copper work for her warships.

Revere had his rolling mill for the manufacture of copper at Canton, a pleasant green village outside of Boston, because he needed waterpower to turn his rolls and press the metal flat. In the summers, he and his family lived there to be near the mill and enjoy the country air. In winter, they lived in Boston, on Charter Street, in a big brick house painted yellow. They were very well off. Now Paul Revere could send his sons to Europe to study metalwork and to see the world, or to Harvard. And his girls could have prettier bonnets and gowns than his own sister had been able to afford at the same age. One luxury Paul Revere had always had, even when he was quite poor, and that was a horse. Now he could have the finest horse he could buy. He often rode back and forth from Canton to Boston on his horse. And he sometimes stopped at the shipyards to see how the frigates were coming along.

The most famous of the new frigates was the *Constitution*. In his shop, Paul Revere had made the metal for her. From his house on Charter Street, he

could see her rising at Hartt's Yard. With her great spread of sail, woven in Boston, her decks of Carolina pitch pine, her red cedar from Savannah and Charleston, her home-manufactured copper, and her flag of fifteen stars, she was a symbol of the young Republic she was so gallantly to defend. She victoriously fought the French, the Algerians, and, during the War of 1812, the English, and won for herself the proud name, *Old Ironsides*.

Paul Revere had many trades — engraving, dentistry, umbrella-mending, money-printing, shopkeeping, the army, designing powder mills, and fitting people to glasses; but there were three in which he excelled: his silver work — no one in America at that time was quite so great an artist in silver; his manufacture of copper; and his casting of bells. Some of his bells were for ships — the *Constitution* had one of them — but most of them were large bells for church steeples. In all, he cast some four hundred for churches, to ring to the glory of God and the memory of Paul Revere. The biggest and most beautiful of all of them was hung in King's Chapel's stone tower in Boston.

When a bell was finished, Revere asked whoever had ordered the bell, to hear it tested. If they did not like the sound, they need not buy. The bell was carted to his back yard, and naturally the small boys wanted to come too. Sometimes they would get too close. Then he would push them aside with his cane. 'Take care, boys! If that hammer hit your head, you'd ring louder than these bells do.' Years later, when these boys were old men, they would remember 'Old Mr. Revere' standing in the sunshine of his garden, testing his bells for the men who came to buy, and watching to see the small boys' heads did not get hit by mistake, instead of the bell.

The bells would be sent inland by ox team or down the coast by sail. There was not one ship except sailing ships in Boston Harbor — so beautiful, white, clean, majestic. But as Revere watched them, he wondered about the future. He was working on some copper boilers for Robert Fulton's 'steam ship,' which might or might not work.

When his children were grown up, and they in turn had children, Paul Revere told stories to his grandchildren at the pleasant house in Canton. Certain things he had seen happen he did not want them to forget.

44

In his lifetime — and he had lived for a long time — there had been almost as many years of war as of peace. And now, thank God, there was peace once more. The country was growing bigger all the time, and Revere was sending bells to far away places he had never heard of when he was his grandchildren's age. The Yankee ships were carrying the American flag with fifteen stars (and maybe sometime there would be some more stars), all over the world. They were also carrying with them some very good Revere copper.

Before the children were sent to bed, he would recite for them a little poem he had recently made up. It was not much of a poem, but it told of waking in the morning to the tune of robin and of wren, and the sound of his forge and the rolling mill, of getting up and taking a walk.

> 'Then round my acres few I trot
> To see what's done and what is not
> Give orders what ought to be done
> And sometimes take my dog and gun.'

His poem tells how on other days he loved to ride out on horseback, or

> . . . Ere the Sun sinks in the West
> Or tuneful birds skim to their nests
> To walk through groves and grassy fields
> Contemplating what nature yields.'

45

He had had a long life and enjoyed it. The last line of his poem was

'We prepare for bed, and so trudge on.'

Then the children would know that was a hint they themselves must now go to bed. For a little longer Paul Revere would sit alone thinking by himself.

46